PASSION *for* FASHION

PASSION *for* FASHION

Careers in Style

JEANNE BEKER

Illustrated by Nathalie Dion

TUNDRA BOOKS

Published in Canada by Tundra Books,
75 Sherbourne Street, Toronto, Ontario M5A 2P9

Published in the United States by Tundra Books of Northern New York,
P.O. Box 1030, Plattsburgh, New York 12901

Library of Congress Control Number: 2007927431

Library and Archives Canada Cataloguing in Publication

Beker, Jeanne
Passion for fashion : Careers in style / Jeanne Beker ; illustrations by Nathalie Dion.

ISBN 978-0-88776-800-2

1. Fashion – Vocational guidance – Juvenile literature. I. Dion, Nathalie, 1964- II. Title.

GT518.B435 2008   J746.9'2023   C2007-902737-7

We acknowledge the financial support of the Government of Canada through the Book Publishing Industry Development Program (BPIDP) and that of the Government of Ontario through the Ontario Media Development Corporation's Ontario Book Initiative.
We further acknowledge the support of the Canada Council for the Arts
and the Ontario Arts Council for our publishing program.

ONTARIO ARTS COUNCIL
CONSEIL DES ARTS DE L'ONTARIO

Medium: Digital

Design: Jennifer Lum

Printed in China

1 2 3 4 5 6   13 12 11 10 09 08

To Mummy – for making my clothes, and believing in me
– J.B.

To Mathilde, my impassioned-for-fashion daughter
– N.D.

"Fashion is not something that exists in dresses only;
fashion is something in the air. It's the wind that blows in the new fashion;
you feel it coming, you smell it . . . in the sky, in the street.
Fashion has to do with ideas, the way we live, what is happening."
– Coco Chanel

Acknowledgments

Fashion's colorful players are a never-ending source of inspiration for me – from the divas to the dressers, the exquisite cast of characters who inhabit my stylish world always amaze me with their unparalleled passion and boundless creativity. I'd like to thank Tundra's Kathy Lowinger for helping me to encourage a whole new generation of fashionistas; my own gorgeous girls, Bekky and Joey, for indulging the fashionista in me; and my dear mother, Bronia, and sister, Marilyn, for fueling my early fashion dreams. I'm also grateful to the following for all their support and inspiration: the late greats Bill Blass, Kal Ruttenstein, and Kevyn Aucoin; *Vogue*'s inimitable André Leon Talley and the *International Herald Tribune*'s Suzy Menkes, from whom I learn so much; my Paris field producer, Shane Hogan, and all my tireless cameramen, especially Jeff Brinkert, Arthur Pressick, Jim Needham, Martin Brown, and Basil Young, who still manage to humor me in the trenches; Marcia Martin and Jay Levine, who got me into the fashion business in the first place; my FT family; my FQ family; Michael King and Geoffrey Dawe; Jessica Fenton; Sue Tate; David Greener; Christopher Sherman; Gregory Parvatan; Carol Leggett; Louise Kennedy; Bonnie Brooks; Penny Fiksel; Jackie Feldman; Deenah Mollin; Kate Alexander Daniels; Mary Symons; Eden del Pilar; and all those beautiful girls and boys backstage who help make the fashion magic.

Introduction
FASHION DREAMS & SCHEMES

Pursuing a whole world of beautiful possibilities

From the very first time I heard about Cinderella's amazing makeover, I've loved fashion's magical possibilities. Fashion can transform you and empower you. It's a wonderful mode of self-expression — and in our increasingly busy society, where we all long for our individual voices to be heard, fashion has become a necessary and valuable tool.

But the world of fashion extends far beyond the obvious. When we think of it, we tend to focus on those images of beautiful clothes created by celebrated designers and worn by gorgeous models, yet there's a whole thriving industry made up of some of the most creative and talented people on the planet. This book opens a window onto the exciting fashion arena and tells you about the many players who make this industry magical.

While fashion has been important to us culturally throughout history, mirroring our lives and times, in the 1960s, we experienced a fashion revolution. Teenagers weren't content to dress anything like their parents and wanted a wild style they could call their very own. We started seeing a new breed of creative designer – those, inspired by music, who really "thought outside the box." They gave us clothing that was artful, spirited, and liberating. From wild colors and psychedelic prints to miniskirts and bell-bottom pants to brave new twists on boring old classics, fashion suddenly became fun and entertaining. And we started thinking in original and colorful new ways.

Not content to follow the crowd and just buy trendy clothing off the rack, I began collaborating with my mother on all kinds of interesting designs, some inspired by my favorite fashion magazines, others by available patterns and fabrics. My patient mom sewed like crazy and made my sister and me small wardrobes of some of the coolest and funkiest clothes imaginable.

Because I had aspired to be an actress, fashion represented costumes to me. I loved dressing according to my mood and felt as though I could change my identity with the way I dressed. Still, as much as I adored fashion, I never dreamed of pursuing a career in it. But life often takes strange twists and turns. And sometimes, if you leave yourself open to all possibilities while pursuing what you *think* you love best, you end up discovering related passions that can be even more fulfilling than anything you ever imagined.

As the host of Fashion Television, I'm proud to say that my team and I have brought the world of fashion into millions

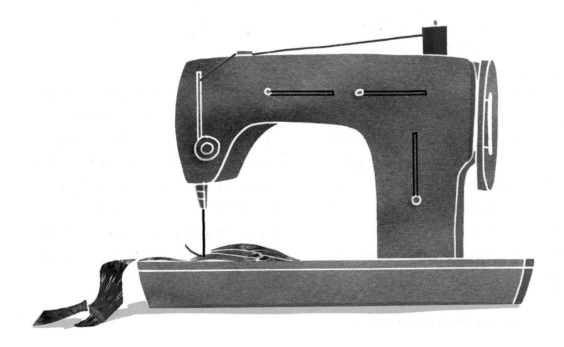

of homes around the globe. A whole generation has grown up watching our weekly show, discovering style and the celebrated personalities – designers, models, and photographers – who make up the scene.

Young people are forever telling me that our show inspired them to pursue careers in fashion. I like to think it's because we've captured so much of the candid behind-the-scenes excitement. Once, fashion was considered a snooty subject, and only those "in the know" about high style and designer fare could really appreciate its inner workings. But now, primarily because of television, designers have become household names, and we follow them in the same way that we follow celebrities from the worlds of music or film.

Fashion, to be sure, is a wild and crazy industry that attracts some of the most imaginative souls. And with all the fantastic runway shows staged around the globe, the ultraexpensive and original ad campaigns, and the fact that great style is now available at reasonable price points, fashion has become a huge multifaceted business – one that offers countless opportunities to those with a passion for creativity, communication, and glamour, who aren't afraid of hard work and big challenges. Fashion is such a fast-paced business that stress levels can run very

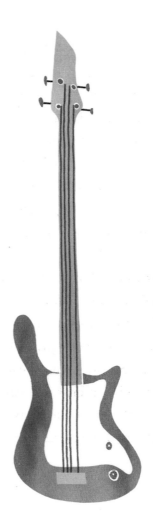

high, but the rewards are phenomenal: from the joy of creative collaboration to the satisfaction of production to the thrill of successful marketing. And while fashion may never change the world, many fashion people have helped to change the *look* of the world and made all our lives a little easier, more fun, and a whole lot more beautiful.

1 DESIGNING YOUR FUTURE

From the drawing board to the runway:
The art and craft of the designer and the business of production

The Designer

While the industry attracts all kinds of creative artists, none are more responsible for the direction of fashion than the designers themselves – those hugely talented men and women who dream up collections of new creations at least every six months and who bravely send them down the runways of the world. Theirs is a life of perpetual inspiration that breeds countless ideas. Part of the art of what they do is deciding which ideas are worth executing into possible new trends. But as brilliant as designers'

ideas may be, unless they have the technical knowledge and expertise to turn their concepts into something both appealing and wearable, they won't get very far. That's why training and on-the-job experience are of utmost importance for a career in fashion design. And because great design usually has its roots in historical research – understanding the fashion of the past and how it can be reinterpreted for the future – a good academic education is also important. Still, all aspiring designers have their own paths. The popular, much-loved, American

> "As difficult as it was to start my career in fashion, I feel it was inevitable. I started by making puppets. It's how I learned to sew, making costumes for puppets – hand puppets and marionettes. I had a huge puppet theater in the garage. It seems like exactly what I do now, only on a different scale.
> – ISAAC MIZRAHI, designer"

designer Betsey Johnson went to Pratt University and then to Syracuse University for three years. But she was an art major. "I never studied fashion design," she says. "I don't think it's necessarily essential to go to a specialized fashion school, but you *must* learn to sew, make patterns, and drape. So it is a good idea to take some 'focused' courses in design and construction. Oh, and you've got to have talent!" she adds. But beyond the technique and the talent, the more you understand the way the world works, the better your contributions are likely to be. After all, besides being esthetically pleasing, great fashion design is meant to make the lives of the men and women who wear the clothes a little easier and more comfortable.

All good designers must also have a unique vision and a sense of style that set them apart. Then there's that inherent passion. I can't think of one designer I've met who wasn't intrigued by clothes from a very young age. America's Michael Kors made little leather vests in his basement when he was a kid. Isaac Mizrahi started his love affair with fashion by making costumes for his puppets. Anna Sui used to make clothes for her Barbie dolls out of Kleenex. And even though Stella McCartney told me that she was a bit of a tomboy growing up, she remembers dressing in her mom's platforms. Then, when she went to work for a Paris designer at the age of fifteen, she really got bitten by the fashion bug. British design genius Alexander McQueen started making clothes when he was about ten years old. And the great Karl Lagerfeld claims he was ultra style-obsessed as a little boy too.

Interestingly, many of the world's top designers have told me that when they were younger, they felt like outsiders. Maybe their highly creative minds were operating on another level, or maybe they were such "original" thinkers, or perhaps even dressers, that they never felt they really fit in with the crowd. Expressing themselves through fashion provided a satisfying sense of independence.

But just as designers must be strong-willed leaders, they also have to be able to work with a collaborative team, as it takes far more than one

Designer
ALEXANDER McQUEEN

*B*orn in London, England, Alexander McQueen left school at age sixteen to apprentice with top Savile Row tailors. He worked with famous theatrical costumiers Angels Fancy Dress, where he mastered six methods of pattern-cutting. At age twenty, he went to work for Japanese designer Koji Tatsuno, and a year later he traveled to Milan and became Romeo Gigli's design assistant.

McQueen returned to London in 1994 and completed his master's degree in fashion at Central Saint Martins College of Art and Design. He began his own successful label upon graduation. From 1996 to 2001, McQueen worked as head designer for the French house of Givenchy. He then went into partnership with the Gucci Group in December 2000. McQueen is now one of the world's most revered designers, and he has been appointed Most Excellent Commander of the British Empire by Queen Elizabeth II.

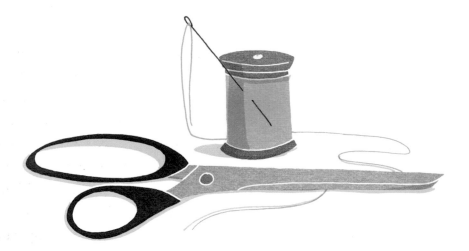

creative person to produce a collection. Aside from the business and marketing people who eventually help get the clothes out there – and whom we'll talk about later on – there are leagues of important production people associated with every successful designer, from design assistants and pattern-makers to sample-makers and seamstresses. It's the duty of these technically proficient workers to help the designer execute his or her vision, and some devoted assistants and head seamstresses are so in synch with the designers they work for that they stay on with them for many, many years. Karl Lagerfeld, at the House of Chanel, fondly talks about one invaluable couture seamstress he's worked with for over thirty years!

The Collections

There are two sides to the high-fashion coin: Ready-to-wear, or "Prêt-à-porter" as they call it in French, and Couture. Ready-to-wear designers do at least two collections a year, for spring/summer and fall/winter. Then many do a "holiday" collection of very fancy pieces. And some may do a "resort" or "cruise" collection, comprised of leisurely, lightweight clothing to be worn in sunny climes. These designers don't get much rest: Almost as soon as one collection is finished, they have to get started on the next. Couturiers specialize in custom-made, one-of-a-kind clothing and often design with a certain individual in mind. Some of the famous design houses in Paris, like Dior and Chanel, have different studios, or "ateliers," that produce both ready-to-wear and couture collections. The couture pieces are exceptionally intricate, ultracostly creations that are worn only by a precious handful of the world's richest women. These expensive made-to-measure confections – worth tens of thousands of dollars – are sometimes never sold, but produced largely for the sake of media attention, which ends up promoting the fashion house. Then the fashion house can sell its more affordable perfumes or handbags. It's all part of the fascinating business strategy of fashion. But not all designers concern themselves with even trying to understand this part of the industry: Many are content with merely creating beautiful garments and, eventually, seeing them worn into the world.

One thing that every designer must have in order to succeed, besides great ideas, technical expertise, a good work ethic, patience, and talent, is tenacity. The fashion business is fraught with rejection and frustration, and sometimes it's that sheer determination to hang on and fight for what you believe in that sees a designer through. Of course, with all the teamwork involved, compromise is often necessary, but it's of paramount importance to keep your nose to the grindstone and never give up. Holding fast to your ideas is admirable and often vital to not only surviving as a designer, but to really making a mark on the world.

While sportswear or eveningwear designers are the most common, more and more designers are specializing in just one area. There are leisurewear designers who create for specific leisure activities, like golf or yoga; lingerie designers; and swim- and beachwear designers. There are millinery designers, like the famous Irish-born Philip Treacy, whose fantasy hats have graced some of the world's most famous heads, from royalty to movie stars. "People who work in the fashion business are attracted to aesthetic," Philip once told me. "And hats are an aesthetic medium. Some of the most aesthetic and beautiful images we've ever had have been hat images. . . . People understand beautiful lines around the face. They're attracted to them. It's a visual experience, whether you're a hat wearer or not."

Shoe designers have also gained a lot of attention, with so many "fashionistas" being shoe-obsessed. Genius footwear aficionados like Christian Louboutin and Manolo Blahnik have become household names. Christian has been fascinated by high-heeled shoes ever since he was a kid. He eventually got a job working with Paris showgirls and began designing footwear especially for them. Manolo started as a fashion illustrator, until the legendary editor of *Vogue* magazine, the late great Diana Vreeland, encouraged him to design shoes. Of course, designing shoes requires very specialized training, and there are several exceptional shoe-design schools that cater to those with a passion for shoe biz. As Manolo Blahnik once told me, "Shoes are the new jewels of our time. If you cannot afford jewels, you can always buy shoes instead."

At one time, most designers were content to work intensely in back rooms for the fashion houses that employed them. But by the 1960s, the idea of the "celebrity designer" emerged. Legendary creators, like France's Pierre Cardin and later America's Calvin Klein, became such powerful forces that they began to be responsible for not only designing the various collections, but also for licensing their names to companies that simply wanted to associate their products with them. Then, in the 1980s, with the popularity of fashion on television and the increasing number of musicians and actresses who forged personal relationships with designers, the designers became celebrities in their own right, just as intriguing as the rock stars they dressed. Take the late Italian-born Gianni Versace – once an aspiring architect, he turned his fashion house into an empire and became as famous for hanging out

with Elton John and throwing fabulous star-studded parties as he was for the fantastic clothing he designed. New York's Isaac Mizrahi, another celebrated designer who always had a penchant for showbiz, even starred in a hit documentary film about his work entitled *Unzipped*, and then, besides designing a mass-produced clothing line, he went on to host a TV talk show.

Of course, this isn't to say that all designers necessarily enjoy being in the spotlight, or that they're all big media stars. Many talented designers are content to simply work hard at what they love and create successful collections. They actually see their media obligations as being a bit bothersome. But the truth is, in order to be a popular, successful designer today, you may have to work at not being shy. Promotion is a very important part of fashion's big picture, as you'll see in chapter four.

As long as you can remain inspired – and that often means traveling to many far-flung places to seek new ideas and fresh ways of looking at the world and the way people move through it – you'll always have something to say as a designer. But a designer without a financial backer – someone to put up the money to run the designer's business – or a manufacturing company or established fashion house to work for won't be able to design much.

The Production Manager and the Sales Agent

Unless designers have the means to independently finance their own businesses, it's important to seek out the right production partners – those who'll be happy taking care of business while the designers concentrate on creative direction. A solid fashion-business team would include a chief financial officer to look after the books, a production manager to take care of getting the product manufactured and shipped, and a salesperson to take charge of getting the right clients who'll place those all-important orders.

While designers themselves are usually the most celebrated figures in fashion and their jobs seem ultimately glamorous, they unquestionably have the toughest job: They have to keep the ideas coming; their work is constantly scrutinized; and they have to work like the devil to get their creations out there and to keep reminding everyone that they're around. Still, when a strong passion to design is coupled with a strong vision and a commitment to work, the rewards of a design career can't be beat.

Alexander McQueen once told me that the best advice he'd give aspiring designers would be to be true to themselves, and to try and maintain their visions at any cost. He added that, most importantly, aspiring young designers have to level with themselves, being honest when assessing how good they really are. If you don't believe you're that good, find something else to do in fashion. But if you really do think that you have what it takes, the fashionably blue sky, my dears, is the limit.

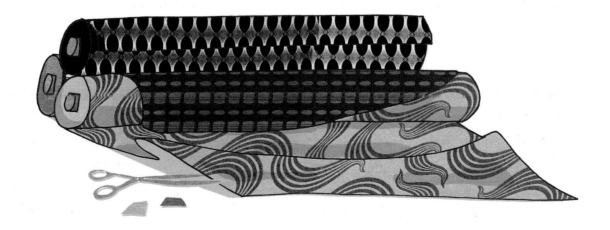

2 MODEL MANIA

Models, agents, and bookers:
The players who strut the stuff and make the scene go round

The Model

The goddesses of the fashion world are undeniably the models – those striking young women who get to strut designers' dreams and become iconic fantasies for fashion's adoring fans. Models are often idolized in our society, and while most barely earn a decent living, some do go on to achieve superstar status. But a lot of pressure goes along with that. Models are constantly being judged and must take exceptional care of their physical selves. Models must also be able to face rejection. They have to be creative, controlled, and self-conscious yet confident at the same time. They must have a unique look and a solid sense of style. But most importantly, they have to be grounded, or the ups and downs of the profession could get to them easily. Famed Brazilian model Gisele Bündchen told me that she's adamant about

treating modeling as a business, and that's helped her. "I'm very professional. I go there, I do my job, I do the best I can, and I go home and I have my life. I have my family, who keeps me grounded, and my friends. I just do a job and I enjoy doing it and it's fun, but it's also fun while I'm out of it. It's good to balance," she confides.

Most models' aspirations to "pose" begin at a fairly young age. If not, and if they're especially attractive, they may simply get "discovered" and be catapulted into this fickle business that's largely about physical appearance. Of course, business-minded models who take what they do seriously can make quite a career for themselves – and that goes for both female and male models. Many male models, however, don't take modeling as a career all that seriously and may see it solely as a travel opportunity or stepping-stone to some other career.

Model
DARIA WERBOWY

*B*orn in the Ukraine, Daria Werbowy moved to Mississauga, Ontario, with her parents when she was three years old. By age fourteen, she was 5'11." Although Werbowy never thought seriously about modeling, she was persuaded to try it out after meeting a schoolmate's mother who headed up a small Toronto agency. A year later, she switched to Elite Models and began to land prominent bookings. When Elite's Elmer Olsen started his own agency, Daria followed him and by 2001, she'd appeared on the covers of *Elle Québec* and *Clin d'oeil*. Shortly afterward, she went national by appearing in an editorial shoot for Canada's *Fashion* magazine; she then went global, appearing on a multitude of covers.

Within a few years, Werbowy has built one of the most enviable resumés in the modeling world, with clients that include Yves St. Laurent, Versace, Marc Jacobs, Louis Vuitton, Gucci, Givenchy, Ralph Lauren, and Christian Dior. Werbowy has also done major campaigns for Chanel and Prada, and she was the face of Lancôme's *Hypnose* perfume.

They tend to have significantly lower day rates, fewer opportunities, and less prestigious jobs than their female counterparts, resulting in less motivation to strive for the top. Still, there are many high-profile and well-paid male models out there, but they're far outnumbered by the young women, or "girls," as they're commonly referred to in the industry.

There are varying opinions on the best time for a model to actually start her career. Some believe every girl should finish high school first; some see it as a great way to pay for college. Lots of girls take time off to model between high school and college. Most start rather young – some as early as fourteen or fifteen. While these young girls might be at the right physical stage, their emotional maturity is paramount to avoiding disaster! There are many perils out there, and a girl must be ultimately responsible for herself. But if she is truly ready to embark on the modeling adventure, it can be a most exciting, challenging, and rewarding career. As it is a fairly short-lived one, I'd encourage every aspiring model to see the profession as a stepping-stone to bigger things. Modeling can open many doors, expose you to all kinds of exciting people and exotic travel, and teach you a lot about the ways of the fashion world – and life in general.

The first thing to do as an aspiring model is to align yourself with a legitimate modeling agency. Be prepared to do a certain amount of research, making sure that the agency is reputable, with a track record of representing models who manage to get work. Any agency that demands that you put out money for either modeling "lessons" or a major portfolio of photographs is possibly questionable. If you do have what it takes, an agency will be only too happy to sign you and send you out on "castings," or auditions, with the expectation of getting a percentage (typically 20-25% or more) of your fees. Sometimes, you may be asked to pose in an "editorial" – a fashion spread in a magazine – for very little, or no money at all. As long as it's for a reputable publication, this is a great opportunity. The more editorial work you have to your credit, the more exposure you'll get, the more impressed potential clients will be, and the more likely you'll land a campaign – and that's where the real money is to be made. The same goes for runway modeling. While some of the

major models can make up to $10,000 a day in an important runway show, other models make runway appearances for little or no money, just to gain experience and exposure.

Sometimes models do have to make an investment in themselves and finance their own trips to foreign countries, where an agency will put them up in models' apartments, with other girls, and

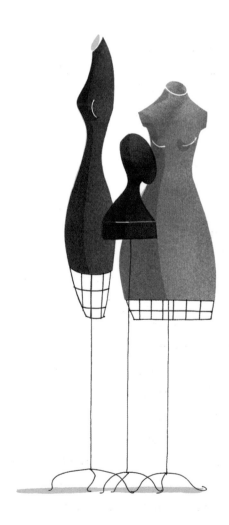

send them out to castings to meet photographers, designers, and magazine editors. This experience can be very enriching – if a girl is mature enough to know how to handle herself. Younger models are often accompanied to foreign locations by chaperones, or even their own mothers! While the fashion world can be ultraglamorous and exciting, it can also be a dark dangerous place, inhabited by shady characters who prey on naïve young girls with stars in their eyes. Be forewarned . . . and be smart about it all.

Most models are required to be a certain height – usually 5'9" at least. But there are always exceptions. There are

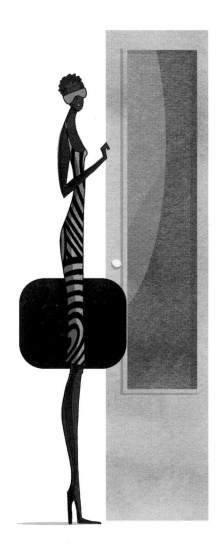

models who may never walk a runway, but who have extremely beautiful faces and get beauty editorials, print campaigns, or commercials. Then there are "parts" models – those with exquisite hands, or feet, or legs. There are also plus-size models, who are increasingly in demand these days. Not every model craves a career in the limelight. Someone with the right proportions might be content being a "fit" model – working with designers and sample-makers as they produce their collections. Fashion showrooms also often employ "showroom" models, who get to strut sample garments only in the privacy of the showroom, as buyers shop through the various collections they want their stores to carry.

Because the business of modeling places so many demands on one's physicality, models have to work especially hard to eat and exercise properly, keeping themselves in top-notch shape. A good model must be extremely disciplined, taking special care to get all the rest she needs and paying attention to her personal grooming, no matter how hectic her schedule. After all, the nature of this ruthless business is largely about presentation, and often, you don't get a second chance. Nobody wants to hear excuses. If you want to be a successful model, you almost have to want it more than anything in the world and

> The most rewarding thing is to take a tall, unpopular girl in high school and transform her into a girl that's a sought-after model, walking runways for the biggest designers.
>
> – ELMER OLSEN, AGENT

work extremely hard at the way you project yourself in front of a photographer, or how you walk down a runway. These days, models must have a wide range of looks and abilities. And while some have lucrative careers merely working for catalogs, most aspire to have a varied experience, from magazines to runways to TV commercials.

Only a precious handful of girls make it big in modeling – the competition is fierce and the nature of the work is merciless, with lots of "hanging around" for your big moment in front of the camera and having all kinds of people fuss over you, primp you, prod you, and generally tell you what to do. It can be very humbling. The business can also get lonely, being "on the road" so much, or in a foreign city for weeks or months on end. The travel opportunities sound exciting at first, but all that jet lag and living in hotel rooms halfway around the world aren't everybody's idea of a good time.

The Agent

If you don't have what it takes to be a model – either physically or psychologically – but are still intrigued by that side of the fashion business, you might consider more of a behind-the-scenes role. Model agents have become very powerful in recent years, and setting up your own agency, or representing a strong stable of models, can be very lucrative. It's almost like being a casting director. As a model agent, you're responsible for "discovering" new girls all the time, and spotting raw talent is a huge talent in itself. This career demands that you keep abreast of all the trends that are happening in the business and cultivate good relationships with a wide array of photographers and magazine editors. It also requires you to have a nurturing personality and the ability to help a girl develop the social maturity and business savvy she'll need to make it. You also have to be extremely organized. But there's a real natural talent in being a good model agent. "You need to have a God-given gift of having the right eye, but you also must be ahead of the trends when it comes to discovering someone," says top Canadian model agent Elmer Olsen, who's helped launch the careers of some the world's top models, including Linda Evangelista. "Then you need the right mix of charisma and personality to build your relationships and keep fostering them through the years."

Another wonderful agent, Calgary's Kelly Streit of Mode Models, who calls himself a "mother" agent, deals with booking his girls through other agencies and discovered and launched the careers of Tricia Helfer, Heather Marks, and Lisa Cant. He says one of the hardest things about his job is the rejection process. "When I have to tell a model that it's just not going to work . . . that's always a little tough. Especially when there are tears. But it's part of what we do, and that's the honesty that's necessary in our business," he says.

The Booker

Model bookers are those who work at the various agencies and send girls out on castings. Theirs is a stationary job that requires them to be on the phone a lot of the time, making connections. But it can also be an exciting "hot seat" to be in, as rewarding as it is stressful. If a girl lands a job, her booker will "book" her and coordinate her schedule. Again, this requires someone with a nurturing, supportive personality, who can be sympathetic to a model, but unwavering in his or her professional commitment to get the job done and keep those all-important clients happy. Very often, though, things fall through at the last minute, and the booker has to scramble to rearrange the model's schedule, or find an appropriate new girl for the job.

Throughout modern fashion history, there have always been stellar models who have greatly inspired designers and captured our imaginations. Some became major celebrities, often frowned upon by serious fashion pundits, who felt nothing should upstage the fashion itself. The concept of the "supermodel" has largely fallen to the wayside, even though some exceptional models – like Britain's Kate Moss, Brazil's Gisele Bündchen, and more recently, Canada's Daria Werbowy and Irina Lazaraneau – will likely always turn heads, and in time, become modern-day legends. Still, the sad truth is, while most talents cannot be compared, no one in this business is irreplaceable. And, as with any trend-driven industry, what or who is hot one minute can quickly cool down the next. The big lesson here is to never take any success for granted.

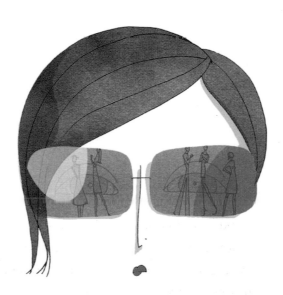

3 PICTURE THIS

The exciting arena of fashion photography

The Photographer

One of the most dynamic, creative, and high-profile arenas in the fashion world belongs to the photographers – those talented men and women who, inspired by the creativity of the designers and the allure of the models, capture the magic and give us memorable images that encourage us to look at the art of fashion in a whole new light. Whether these photographers shoot fashion for art's sake, create provocative ad campaigns, or work with editors to tell intriguing stories on the pages of fashion magazines, their inspired missions are laborious and painstaking. It's as though they're directors on a movie set, working closely with their creative "crew," or team, in an effort to create perfection. They must have a strong vision, a great understanding of the clothes themselves, a sensitivity to the "story" that the magazine editor or advertising client wants to tell, and, above all, an ability to clearly direct the model, the stylist, the makeup and hair people, and their own assistants. A photo shoot is a highly collaborative operation, where stress levels often run high. But the excitement and exhilaration from an inspired session are beyond compare and make all the meticulous, detailed hard work so very worthwhile.

A great fashion photographer must have a solid technical background. Though some may claim to be self-taught, having picked up a camera at a young age, it's best to study photography at a reputable school and really learn the ins and outs of the entire creative and technical process. Knowledge of lighting is paramount, and understanding what works best in various conditions and for different effects, coupled with an intimate knowledge of equipment and developing techniques, will serve you well. Of course, more and more, fashion photographers are veering away from using film and are relying on digital means to capture and produce their images. While working with old-fashioned film can be artistically satisfying, so much more magic is possible using digital cameras that many photographers and editors prefer them. Besides all the special effects you can create, the results are visible instantaneously.

In the high-pressure world of magazines, where time is always of the essence, that is a godsend.

Since fashion photographers spend a lot of their time shooting beautiful clothing, it's important for them to have a strong appreciation for it and to know what styles, fabrics, and colors shoot best. But they don't necessarily have to be well-versed in terms of designers. They usually have stylists at their side, choosing the clothes, dressing the model, and suggesting styling possibilities.

Photographer MARIO TESTINO

Born in Lima, Peru, Mario Testino attended the American School of Lima, and then studied economics at the University del Pacífico, law at the Universidad Católica, and international relations at the University of San Diego, California. He moved to London in 1976 and began his formal training in photography. Testino now travels extensively for American, British, French, and Italian *Vogue*, and *Vanity Fair*. He has photographed many celebrities, from Madonna to the late Diana, princess of Wales; contributed to images of leading fashion houses, such as Givenchy, Christian Lacroix, Valentino, Gucci, Yves St. Laurent, Versace, and Calvin Klein; and photographed several beauty and fragrance campaigns, including Gucci, Valentino, and Shisheido.

Testino published his first book of photography, *Any Objections?*, in 1998, and several others followed, including *Front Row/Backstage*, *Alive*, and *Kids*. Solo exhibitions of his work have been mounted in cities such as Tokyo, Naples, Sao Paolo, New York, London, Brussels, and Stockholm. Testino is one of the world's most sought-after photographers in fashion today.

The photographer, however, is ultimately the one in charge of the set and what goes on there. And while art directors, editors, or other clients may be present, most seasoned photographers request – and receive – a fair amount of creative input and control, as long as they're ultimately giving the art director, editor, or client what they want. Even though some photographers are famous for their huge egos, the best in the business realize that the art of fashion photography is largely a collaborative process, and it's important to keep everyone involved passionate about the work at hand in order to get the best results.

True magic can happen in a photo if the photographer knows how to direct his or her model. Making a strong connection is imperative – it's the photographer and the model who often inspire each other to great heights. Of course, fashion photographers get offered all kinds of assignments, and some are unquestionably more "artistic" than others. Most working photographers can't always afford to pick and choose what they want to shoot – not until they become famous. But true fashion photography – beyond the purely commercial images we see in catalogs – has become a well-respected art form, and many famous fashion photographers end up doing their own books, or having exhibitions in art galleries.

Then, as their star rises, they can be much more selective about their work. But building a profile as a great fashion photographer can take years of hard work and dues-paying. The best fashion photographers in the world are the ones that develop a particular style or vision for which they are known. They also have good relationships with magazine editors and art directors in order to be offered work in the first place. Because fashion photography has been so glamorized in the media, it's becoming an increasingly popular career choice. But it is a tough road, and only those passionate people with incredible tenacity, who are willing to work very hard and to compromise to

some degree, have a real chance of making it. Working well with others is a main component to success.

The Photographer's Assistant

Every photographer must have one or more reliable assistants, whether working digitally or with film. These assistants are often aspiring photographers themselves and see their work as great experience — the perfect preparation for one day becoming full-fledged photographers themselves. The photographer's assistant has to do everything, from loading the camera (if it's a shoot that's using film) to getting light levels to setting up backdrops. Being a photographer's assistant can be a demanding job, but a rewarding and educational one, learning the art and craft of photography firsthand, on professional shoots that really matter.

The Producer

Another key job in the field of fashion photography is that of the producer, the person employed by the magazine or advertising client who pulls all the elements of the shoot together — from finding the location to sometimes suggesting and always booking the photographer, models, hair and makeup people, and stylist. It's imperative for producers to have good relationships with the photographers' agents, the modeling agencies, and those agencies that represent the hair and makeup people. If travel is involved, the producer makes all the arrangements, from flights and car rentals to hotels. The producer also orders the food for the crew on set and is responsible for getting all the permits needed for the shoot, which sometimes involves wading through bureaucratic red tape! For example, if you wanted to shoot at the Eiffel Tower,

> There are many great fashion photographers. What they have in common is a unique vision. Some may call it style, but I feel it's more complex than that. Techniques may go in and out of style, but a unique vision does not.
> — GABOR JURINA, photographer

or on the streets of Manhattan, you'd need clearance from the local government office. Those permits sometimes require a lot of "wheeling and dealing," so you have to have a great deal of patience and go through the right channels.

A producer's job is very hands-on. Besides all the preproduction organization and juggling of the budget, he or she is usually on set all day, solving problems. All the producers I know say it's an exhilarating job, with lots of pressures and responsibilities. But people who become producers generally love troubleshooting and see their work as a series of challenges that they take great delight in overcoming.

While the photographer is a key player in every fashion shoot, he or she doesn't usually have final say in which photo is chosen to be published. Certainly, every good photographer has his or her own idea of which shot they'd like to see used, but photographers are generally required to submit a number of choices, and then an editor-in-chief, creative or art director, or client, has final say. It's not an easy pill for some of the world's most famous photographers to swallow. But then again, as long as someone else is paying the bills, there are often compromises. Many high-end fashion photographers have close and special relationships with the clients or magazines they shoot for, and a few demand, and receive, carte blanche when it comes to making big creative decisions.

4 CREATING THE BUZZ

Getting the word out

Public Relations and Publicity

The pop culture landscape has become a blur of brands – most of them fashion-related. Everybody seems to be working overtime to grab our attention and get their message out there. The good news is, fashion imagery is now increasingly sophisticated, and there are some brilliant and imaginative people in the fashion marketing field, with millions and millions of dollars spent on advertising and promotion each year. These days in fashion, it's largely about brand visibility. People have become label-obsessed, and promoting designer names has developed into a huge and lucrative business. The field of fashion public relations and publicity is highly creative and demanding, with no tolerance for those who aren't prepared to give 100%.

There's no end to the attention to detail, personal politics, and sometimes cutthroat, always competitive spirit inherent in this end of the business. And there's no question that it takes a certain kind of person to really succeed.

The business of public relations and publicity is all about people. Being a clearheaded, creative thinker who's able to communicate effectively with others is paramount. Working in public relations for a fashion company or design house is a taxing and crucial job. Not only are you responsible for presenting the image of the label or the

> "While fashion PR does have its glamorous side (i.e., working with famous celebrities, fancy black-tie parties, international travel, the designer wardrobe), the day-to-day reality is a bit less glam and more about long hours, stressful deadlines, and expert multitasking! To be an effective PR professional, you have to be able to think on your feet, be a polished communicator, a people person by nature, [and] an idea person who understands the bigger picture. It helps to be well versed in art, film, music, literature . . .
>
> — LISA SCHIEK,
> COMMUNICATIONS DIRECTOR, TOM FORD INTERNATIONAL

designer to the world, but you must also deal with all the clients, individual customers, and the media at large. While many successful people in this field work themselves up in big fashion PR companies – some starting with jobs as simple, but personable, as that of receptionist – it's advisable to study communications at a postsecondary institution. Courses in marketing are helpful for this career path as well, since you'll need to understand strategies for getting messages out. A degree in journalism is also highly advantageous. These days, the competition for PR jobs is fierce, and the more you can hone your business and writing skills, the better.

Although writing may not be mandatory in every PR or publicity job, honing this skill is a big plus. You may often have to correspond on behalf of the company or designer you're representing, and since you'd be dealing with the media, that might also include writing press releases. It really helps to have a keen grasp of how journalists and their publications work – that will assist you in getting your message across to them and in "pitching" ideas, as publicists often do. There's an inordinate amount of telephone work in public relations, so you need a good telephone manner. You also have to enjoy taking meetings; going to business-related breakfasts, lunches, dinners, and cocktail parties; and corresponding in general. You have to really like people, be very sociable, and be good at communicating, or this job isn't for you. That's especially important if the designer or fashion company you work for presents fashion shows. It's often up to the PR team to help decide who gets invited and where they sit – and then there are always those haughty guests who get upset with where they're sitting! You've also got to be extremely organized and a diplomat, solving problems and organizing media interviews for your clients. Keep well informed, too, of what's going on in the fashion world – and pop culture in general. Public relations firms and publicists have to ensure that the companies or designers they represent are relevant and interesting to those who are covering them in the media, or to the customers who are buying their products.

While publicists and PR representatives essentially do the same sort of job – promote products or people – those who work for PR companies are generally part of a team. And that team gets involved with many aspects of the fashion company's or designer's image – from strategizing promotions to party planning to running interference with the media (meaning, dealing with the press and sorting out any problems). Publicists are often one-man or one-woman operations, focused on getting the designer or the fashion company exposure and building brand and image awareness. It behooves any PR company or publicist to have strong connections and relationships with newspaper and

magazine journalists, TV producers, and reporters, since "contacts" in the business are so valuable. "And you always need to maintain these relationships," says New York power publicist Lizzie Grubman, "because you never know when you'll need them." The PR representatives of big fashion labels also have to cultivate good relationships with the publicists of celebrities, since designers garner so much attention these days by getting their clothes on the right backs. If a movie star wears a certain label to a red-carpet event and gets photographed, the publicity is invaluable – you can't buy that kind of press! The careers of many designers have been launched by simply having the opportunity to dress the right stars. And that is something the designer's publicist or PR team can often facilitate. Lebanon's Elie Saab, a wonderful designer, was practically unheard of in North America until Halle Berry wore his creation at the Oscars the year she won for Best Actress. Elie became instantly famous!

In order to do a really good job in PR, it's essential to believe in the product, brand, or person you're promoting. That will make your job of "selling" your client to the press and the public much easier. Be conscientious and detail-oriented. And there is no room for mistakes. One of the most stressful aspects of the job is never knowing for sure how your "story" is going to come out in the press. So the big challenge is to try and make sure that your clients are seen in the most positive light.

Publicists and PR people also have to be extremely tenacious. That means not giving up just because your calls aren't returned. Of course, no one wants to make a pest of themselves, but you have to be relentless. And if, for example, the journalist you're trying to pitch a story to won't "bite," you'll have to come up with an irresistible angle. That's why it's important to have an intimate knowledge of the product or person you're promoting, and to be passionate about them. Ultimately, you always have to think fast – and creatively. The rewards, of course, are major: Imagine seeing a huge magazine story that you helped generate, or realizing that it was your hard work that helped create a "buzz" about a certain label or designer.

Publicist
Karla Otto

Born in Bonn, Germany, Karla Otto began modeling while studying in Tokyo, and it was her introduction to the fashion world. In the late '70s, she worked in the PR department of Elio Fiorucci's fashion label in Italy and, after several years with the brand, she decided to set up her own public relations company in Milan. Among her first clients were Jean Paul Gaultier, Prada, Jil Sander, and Marni, and she was instrumental in their development as brands. Otto has organized presentations, parties, and openings for Fendi, Swarovski, Marc Newson, Dom Perignon, Philippe Starck, Villa Moda, Baccarat, and Absolut Vodka. Her client list includes such iconic fashion labels as Christian Dior, Emilio Pucci, Viktor & Rolf, Hussein Chalayan, Calvin Klein, Givenchy, and Valentino. Karla Otto has opened an office in Paris and one in London. A New York branch opened in May 2007.

5 TELLING STORIES

Capturing the magic with journalism and illustration

The Journalist

Perhaps the most powerful force in fashion is the media. Journalists often have the ability to make or break a designer's career, and many of us have learned so much about fashion simply from all the information that we're constantly bombarded with from a wide variety of media outlets. Up until the mid-1980s, most people got their "fashion fix" from magazines and newspapers. Then Fashion Television came along, turning the TV cameras onto the exciting fashion scene in an entertaining way. Viewers had a window onto the glamorous world of gorgeous models, creative personalities, and colorful behind-the-scenes goings-on, which, until that point, had been covered only in the print medium. Suddenly, people all over the planet were privy to a fashionable slice of pop culture. Young and old alike, who normally would never pick up a fashion magazine or the fashion section of a newspaper, were suddenly being exposed to very high doses of style. Television educated its audience to become more style-savvy, and people started to dress better as they learned more about the fascinating designers, their catwalk creations, and how the enigmatic fashion business works.

The Writer and The Critic

Most writers that report on fashion are specialists. They've spent years studying fashion on their own, or at school, and have a keen sense of the nature of the business. The best fashion print journalists are very skilled writers that are able to capture the color and excitement of the scene and translate it onto the printed page. Because the nature of fashion is so visual, that's not an easy thing to do. Fashion writers must paint brilliant pictures for their readers and know how to analyze trends, so that readers can comprehend what comes down the runways of the world. Studying journalism is almost imperative these days. Because so many of us have a strong penchant for fashion, a glamorous and international industry, all kinds of talented young people are vying to get into the field of fashion journalism. Having strong writing skills is a must, along with a knowledge of fashion history – the more we know about where society has come from, the more we understand where it is going. Fashion journalists need frames of reference to be

Journalist
JEANNE BEKER

*B*orn in Toronto, Ontario, Jeanne Beker began acting at the age of sixteen. In the early '70s, she studied acting at the Herbert Berghoff Studio in New York, mime with Étienne Decroux in Paris, and theater at Toronto's York University. In 1975, Beker landed her first media job with CBC Radio in St. John's, Newfoundland, as an arts reporter/documentary producer. She then became a features reporter/producer for Toronto's Chum Radio. In 1979, she launched and co-hosted the groundbreaking TV series *The New Music* at Toronto's City TV and began entertainment reporting on City Pulse News. Beker also helped launch MuchMusic in 1983, where she anchored the news desk, and Fashion Television in 1985, which is now seen in over one hundred countries.

Beker began writing a column in Canada's *Flare* magazine in the early '90s, and she launched @fashion, the first fashion site on the Internet. She began writing a style column for Canada's Southam, Inc. newspapers in 1999 and moved the column to *The Globe and Mail* in 2003. That year, Beker also launched *FQ Magazine*, where she is editor-in-chief, then *SIR Magazine* in 2005. Jeanne Beker is currently the co-creator and co-executive producer of *Cover Stories*, a syndicated documentary TV series about the behind-the-scenes workings of *FQ* and *SIR* magazines. She is also a celebrated judge on *Canada's Next Top Model*.

able to see where a designer's vision fits into the big fashion picture. For critics — those who assess designers' collections and pass judgment on how valid their visions are and how relevant their clothes are — a broad knowledge of fashion and its role in society is imperative. Trends in clothing say a lot about our life and times, and the best fashion critics teach us why certain styles come back and why some styles are more appropriate for the mass-market buyer than others.

The TV Reporter

When I started reporting fashion on TV back in 1985, there was only one other person doing that job full-time in the North American market — a New Zealand native named Elsa Klensch, who'd worked as a fashion magazine editor for years and who was well respected by designers and the industry in general. She reported on international fashion for CNN in a newsy, no-nonsense way. Klensch really knew her stuff, but her focus was reporting on runway trends. My aim, and the aim of my Fashion Television producers, though, was to report on the fashion scene as entertainment. Covering the big international runway spectacles in this lighthearted way, and reporting on the models and designers as celebrities, hadn't

been done before. We were the first, and in a way, invented a new approach to fashion coverage.

It can be very satisfying to communicate ideas about style and trends as a bonafide fashion journalist. Back in the early '90s, I created the first fashion magazine on the Internet. It was called @fashion and featured designer and model profiles, trend reports, style advice, and interviews. Now, fashion on the Net is everywhere, with countless sites devoted to the subject. It's nice to see there's a whole new medium for it — and some of the best fashion writers around, like Tim

Blanks, the former host of another fashion TV series, *Fashion File*, is currently associated with style.com, one of the best fashion sites on the Internet. The appeal of fashion on the Net is that it is instantaneous, with pictures and reports going into cyberspace almost immediately.

The Illustrator

Another form of fashion reportage – and one that could be seen as the most purely artistic – is illustration. Before the advent of fashion photography, illustrators were largely responsible for showing the public what the designers were up to. Illustrators were gainfully employed in the advertising field

> **It helps to understand clothing, from its concept to its construction, to really illustrate fashion well. The other ultimate goal is to create a clear graphic identity or identities, something which becomes a signature style or styles, recognizable as only your work.**
>
> – RICHARD GRAY, fashion illustrator

as well. Now, fashion illustration is making a comeback, and some artists, like the wonderful Ruben Toledo – whose work is featured regularly in impressive ads for the American retailer Nordstrom – are having a huge impact on our style sensibility.

Many multitalented designers manage to do their own sketches, or illustrations, and that's often where the early ideas for their creations come out. But there are lots of great designers who can't draw, so they employ talented illustrators to help them with this very important first stage of creation. Most successful illustrators have studied art formally and are able to not only draw well technically, but to impart an attitude and spirit in their often-quick sketches. Sometimes, at the big fashion shows, you see illustrators sitting with their sketchbooks, simply drawing what they see coming down the runway. Others, like the brilliant and famous

San Francisco based illustrator Gladys Perint Palmer, have little cameras with them. She snaps pictures and then goes home to draw the images she's captured, interpreting them in spirited, insightful ways. Her illustrations have been featured in many books and magazines, as well as in such newspapers as London's *Sunday Times*.

The Editor

Often, fashion journalists become editors — those men and women with such a broad knowledge of fashion that they're able to pick and choose which stories, collections, and personalities are worthy of coverage in style sections of newspapers, or in magazines. There is no set route for training as an editor; every one takes a different path. The broader your experiences and historical references in the fashion industry, the better the editor you likely will be. Some editors are amazing writers; others can't write at all. But it's an intellectual understanding of fashion, an emotional passion for the subject, and a driven personality that are key to an editor's success. Fashion editors are among the most powerful players in the industry, and their personal and professional tastes end up influencing society and promoting various trends. But editors work in a collaborative arena — they're ringleaders in a sense, often toiling alongside a publication's creative director and working with teams of editorial assistants, writers, art directors, photographers, and stylists. Editors usually feel like they're in the eye of the storm, and in the ever-swirling, electric world of fashion, that is an exhilarating place to be.

editor in chief

creative director

beauty editor

fashion director

art director

market editor

sitting editor

managing editor

6 THE GLOSSIES

The intriguing world of fashion magazines

Fashion magazines occupy a special place in the hearts of those of us who adore fashion. Besides providing practical style information, the world's fashion glossies are chock-full of inspiring images and offer food for dreaming. But the fashion magazine arena is an odd and multifaceted one – and success depends on being able to straddle the delicate line between art and commerce. It's one thing to be wildly creative, but if your magazine isn't getting the support it needs from advertisers, your business just won't fly.

While many of the highly artistic people who work at fashion magazines aren't always happy about compromising, that "give-and-take" mentality is mandatory if you want to succeed at a fashion publication. If the sales team isn't able to sell advertising pages, there won't be the editorial pages necessary to get your ideas across, in feature stories or pictures. The more revenue, or income, from ads sold, the more funds the magazine has to hire good writers and photographers.

The Publisher

At the helm of any fashion magazine are the publishers – those people who concern themselves with the big business-picture, trying to make their enterprises lucrative and productive. As passionate as we all are about the highly competitive fashion magazine business, I doubt there's anyone out there who's in it for the "good of their health." It's a tough arena, and you have to be prepared for hard work and commitment. Publishers must have excellent relationships with advertisers – both the actual clients and the media-buying companies that spend the clients' money and place those all-important ads. There's lots of "schmoozing" and socializing because influential contacts are key. Publishers are also responsible for hiring the creative team who dreams up and produces each issue, so they need a good eye for talent, the ability to "lure" the right people, and great business and communication skills.

The Editor-in-Chief

The top jobs at most fashion magazines belong to the editors-in-chief, and sometimes, particularly at large fashion magazines, there are creative directors. When a creative director is on staff, it's imperative for him or her to have a strong working relationship with the editor-in-chief, as, together, they decide on the direction, look, and feel of each issue of the magazine. An editor-in-chief usually wields a lot of power — especially if his or her publication is well distributed and widely read. These top well-respected editors can pick up on ideas and turn them into huge trends. For international fashion publications, they usually travel to the world's fashion capitals and take in all the exciting runway shows, as well as meeting the designers and encouraging their talent. Editors-in-chief must be well connected and well informed of the world around them — it's very often their perspectives that get translated onto the pages of the magazine. That's why they have the luxury of assembling their own "dream" teams and carefully choosing the talents that will help mastermind their vision. "The joy of editing is making the most of people's talents," says Glenda Bailey, editor-in-chief of America's *Harper's Bazaar*, one of the world's most successful fashion magazines. "My job is to make sure that the creative is exquisite and that the words set the agenda for today, all the while keeping in mind that we're creating the history of tomorrow." The editor-in-chief must also work closely with the publisher, to ensure they're "on the same page" when making business and creative decisions. The job requires self-confidence, conviction, a great imagination, a natural curiosity about fashion, the ability to be a good listener, and perhaps most of all, a strong point of view. Because their role is such a public one, they're compelled to be out and about — attending fashion events, supporting the fashion community at large, and

*B*orn in Darby, England, Glenda Bailey entered a business studies course in 1977 and completed her A-Levels in English and economics. In 1979, she studied art and design at Blackpool College, then veered into fashion design at Kingston University in 1980. Upon graduating in 1984, Bailey designed knitwear outside of Milan and then returned to London, where she got a job as a fashion forecaster with Design Direction. There she learned about layouts, copy reviewing, and dealing with clients. In 1986, Bailey landed a job doing a "dummy" of a fashion publication, which became a quarterly called *Folio*. In 1988, she became editor-in-chief of Britain's *Marie Claire* magazine and, in 1992, international editorial director for all *Marie Claire* magazines. Bailey moved to New York in 1996, where she became editor-in-chief of American *Marie Claire*. In 2001, she was appointed editor-in-chief of *Harper's Bazaar*.

frequently taking meetings with potential sponsors and clients. Their image is of utmost importance: They are, in a sense, the face of the magazine, and their attitudes set the tone for the magazine's mind-set.

It can take years to work your way up to a top editor-in-chief position. Most people who've climbed their way up the publishing ladder started as editorial assistants or junior writers, slowly learning editing skills. But not all editors-in-chief necessarily do that. Some arrive at the helm of a magazine because of their high profile and major achievements in a related field. Glenda Bailey urges people not to be afraid to start at the top. "If you're sure of what you want to do," she says, "it's easy to convince others. Just focus on the one thing you really want to do and be strategic," she advises. But because the stakes are so high, only the strong survive. There's little room for error in the publishing business, and if the magazines don't sell, the editors-in-chief often get the blame.

The Creative Director

The creative director must have a mega-imagination, the ability to create magic, and the power to motivate the magazine's art department to come up with inspiring and original layouts. Working closely with the magazine's editor-in-chief, creative directors help formulate the vision and feel of the publication and usually have a strong background in art and design. Generally, the broad concepts for those all-important cover shots come from the editor-in-chief and the creative director.

The Art Director

The art director is also key to a magazine's look and feel, responsible to both the editor-in-chief and the creative director, if there is one. The art director's job is to suggest ways of presenting creative concepts, and then to place these ideas and pictures on the page. Art directors have to have a good eye for graphics and pay extreme attention to detail. The great ones have an uncanny ability to "think outside the box" and come up with creative solutions to all kinds of design challenges. They work with copy provided by the various writers and editors and find the best way of presenting it to the reader. They're instrumental to the photo shoots, often finding the necessary photographers and models for the story and taking an active role in directing the actual shots. These talented people take the editor-in-chief's

*B*orn in Antony, France, Fabien Baron studied at Arts Appliqués in Paris. In 1975, he took a job in the art department at *L'Équipe* magazine, and, in 1982, moved from Paris to New York, where he worked at *Self* and *GQ* magazines. He was then appointed creative director of Italian *Vogue*, moving between New York and Milan. In 1990, he opened his company, Baron & Baron, and guided the relaunch of *Interview* magazine. In 1992, he became the creative director of *Harper's Bazaar*, and he has designed ad campaigns for leading names in fashion, such as Issey Miyake, Hugo Boss, Giorgio Armani, Valentino, Pucci, Michael Kors, and Norma Kamali. He was also creative director for Calvin Klein.

Baron has been involved in monumental projects, such as Madonna's book, *Sex*, the design of Robert Altman's book, *Prêt-à-Porter*, and graphic entities for the Ian Schrager Company. He is currently creative director of French *Vogue*.

and creative director's dreams and spin them into realities on the page.

A successful art director has varied technical skills and a strong background in art and design. These days, most design is done on the computer, so a wealth of computer skills is an asset. Art directors always have to be thinking of new ways to get ideas across and excite the magazine's readers. Above all, they have to be team players. There's no room for diva behavior in the art department of a magazine; the work is too demanding, difficult, and relentless. Sometimes, before you're even finished one issue, you're laying out, or coming up with ideas for, the next. It can be a dizzying environment, but overwhelmingly satisfying. There's nothing like executing ideas on the printed page, while getting accolades for beautiful work from readers, colleagues, and other industry professionals.

The Managing Editor

For those who are more business-minded, the role of managing or executive editor might appeal. These powerful editors run the daily business of the magazine, making sure stories get assigned and filed on time. They are constantly working with deadlines and managing the magazine's eclectic staff. Good managing editors are always in touch with their editors-in-chief, even when the

editors-in-chief are away on magazine business. They juggle budgets and make sure the freelance staff get paid. Once all the ideas, stories, and pictures are laid out, the actual production of the magazine is handled by production managers, who work closely with the printers.

Editors and Editorial Assistants

There are a wide variety of editorial positions available at a fashion magazine, from those bright and eager young interns who often work without pay for the invaluable experience (which often involves doing such menial tasks as going on a coffee run for the editor-in-chief!) to the editorial assistants who make sure that their editor bosses are being placated to an assortment of editors who head up the various departments. Most fashion magazines have a *fashion director*, or *fashion editor*, who's largely responsible for the clothing and accessories the magazine chooses to feature. Fashion directors or editors work closely with stylists on the editorial fashion shoots, suggesting which collections to pull from. They also report on international runway trends, and many travel to see the international collections and visit designer showrooms to see what's in store. Most fashion editors write their own copy — and all must have an analytical mind, understanding which trends are important and which ones are appropriate for their specific readers. Fashion editors work closely with their editors-in-chief, sharing information and helping to come up with creative story ideas about fashion. Each issue usually features one big photographic "trend" story, and the trend that is going to be featured, along with the clothes and accessories to be shown, is often the result of the fashion director's or editor's input. Fashion editors must have a broad understanding of fashion and a keen interest in keeping abreast of what's hot and happening in the fashion world — from what the designers are doing to what the stores are selling to what women are wearing. They must be sensitive to their readers' wants and needs and be able to impart information, and possibly advice, in a comprehensive, engaging way. Some fashion editors are great writers and are responsible for their own copy. Others simply focus on the fashion direction of their publication and leave the writing to other talented staff or freelance journalists.

Market editors do a lot of running around, visiting designers' showrooms and pulling clothes for shoots for the magazine. They attend many fashion shows, always keeping informed of the new trends that are coming down the runways.

Often, freelance stylists are used at magazines, who can be extremely influential in the choice of clothing to be shot. They also do a lot of the running around to find just the right pieces. But the larger magazines have their own market editors, who have a broad knowledge of all the fashion possibilities.

> "I think it takes . . . courage to be an editor because the world (from advertisers, to corporate people, to your staff and writers and photographers) can be pushing you in one direction — but you must be the ultimate advocate for your reader. That can be challenging.
> — ATOOSA RUBENSTEIN, PAST EDITOR-IN-CHIEF, *Seventeen* MAGAZINE

Sittings editors work closely in the field with the creative team — like the art director

and the photographer. They're there largely to oversee everything, especially when a celebrity or high-profile person is being shot as the model. Sittings editors are ultimately responsible for ensuring that everything goes smoothly on the shoot, and their creative input is usually much appreciated, or even heavily relied upon. These editors often travel, jetting off to exotic locations with their teams to get the most beautiful pictures possible.

Beauty editors concentrate on hair, makeup, skin care, fragrance, and other cosmetic trends. They have to be on the cutting edge of all new developments and products in this highly competitive, fast-changing arena and are often invited to attend product launches and seminars. Beauty editors are responsible for informing their editors-in-chief about beauty trends and keeping the rest of the creative teams at the magazines aware of what's new. Beauty editors also help come up with beauty-related stories and have a say in the beauty direction, such as hair and makeup, for editorial fashion shoots. While some beauty editors write a lot, many do not and simply oversee the work of staff or freelance writers. They have to be very detailed-oriented, ensuring that all products used by the hair and

makeup people on the models in the shoots are properly credited. Beauty and cosmetic companies are extremely important advertisers for fashion magazines, and great pains sometimes must be taken to please those clients who are buying the ads.

The biggest challenge for everyone who works in magazines can often be maintaining journalistic integrity, which means truthfulness. But that kind of "honesty" in the fashion business – particularly in the area of journalism – can be a tricky thing. No one wants to offend anybody, but people in this business are frequently highly sensitive. So it's imperative to be diplomatic in the way you deal with others, while at the same time being true to yourself. At the end of the day, it's your professional credibility – that is, your trustworthiness and reliability – that's the most important thing in the fashion business. It's something you have to maintain at all costs, or you'll never be taken seriously or be able to realize your dreams.

7
SHOWTIME!

The almighty fashion show and the people behind the scenes

The Fashion Show

One of the most thrilling and glamorous spectacles in our culture is the fashion show – from the backstage designer dramas and the buzz of the models being primped and preened to the "front-of-house" preparations with the colorful front-row guests and the paparazzi scrambling to get their shots. Once confined to the intimacy of a Paris design house's swish salon, these days fashion shows are being staged in cities the world over and in an endless assortment of venues – from shopping malls and department stores to theaters and opera houses to restaurants and nightclubs. And these shows come in all shapes and sizes, whether they're presented as gala charity benefits or used to promote a retailer's merchandise. Many designers depend on these runway spectacles to get the media attention they crave; and

editors, reporters, and critics scout the catwalks to discover what's new and what's next. Besides being a great showcase for designer fare, the runways are the perfect platform for new model talents, and many photographers attend the international collections specifically to scout new faces.

Retail buyers are also important guests at the designers' shows. While they usually do get a sneak preview of the collections at a designer's showroom, or are invited there to "shop" for their stores and see the clothes up close, it's the runway presentations that often get them excited: This is where the world gets to see the designer's complete vision, and the way in which the clothes are presented on the catwalk can often make or break a designer's success.

No matter how large – and some of these megashows can cost a million dollars or more to stage – or how small, every fashion show needs a good producer or production company behind it. Together with the designer or fashion house's PR people, these producers mastermind and present the actual show, often taking care of every little detail – from choosing the venue to providing the right staging, lighting, and special effects; to booking the models and coordinating the hair and makeup teams; to organizing any backstage managers, assistants, and all the dressers. They make sure the clothes arrive on time and occasionally help organize what takes place front of house. They may also book a choreographer to show the models how to walk. Choreographers that specialize in the art of walking down a runway are often former models themselves. They require an intimate knowledge of body language, a creative take on runway theatrics, and an impeccable sense of timing.

Stylists are also mandatory behind the scenes at fashion shows. They assist the designer with determining the way the models are dressed, and they choose the accessories. With the bigger shows, designers work directly with music directors, who help find just the right music to play as the girls strut their stuff.

The Show Producer

Producing a fashion show can be extremely stressful, since there's so much riding on its success. But Alexandre de Betak, whose Paris-based company *Bureau Betak* produces some of the biggest fashion shows for some of the world's most famous designers, says that stress is only there when he starts a project, three to six months in advance of the show. "That's when I have to find an idea that will help the designer and the show. But when the idea is executed, when it comes to the day of the show, I'm never stressed at all."

Problem-solving is a huge part of the show producer's job, though Alexandre says that "problem anticipating" is what's really necessary – foreseeing each and every problem that might crop up and

> " I start working with the designers [on their next show] pretty much the day after their previous show. . . . We have to start on anticipating production, and the venues, even before they start designing clothes. That's part of what makes it so exciting. "
> – ALEXANDRE DE BETAK, fashion show producer

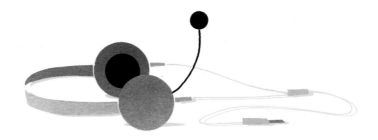

trying to eliminate it before it arises. Surprisingly, most of the really big shows staged during Fashion Weeks in international fashion capitals, like New York, Paris, London, or Milan (and, more recently, in other far-flung cities, such as Medellin, Bombay, Toronto, Hong Kong, Lisbon, Sydney, and beyond), last only about fifteen to twenty minutes. So show-producing is essentially about the preparation – the planning and the organization. Because of all the creative experts that a producer has to assemble and the number of original ideas the production company has to come up with for every single show, some say that the job of a show producer is one of the most creative, exciting, and challenging in the business.

Imagine a designer who wants his models to walk on water, or fly through the air as the great British designer Alexander McQueen once did. Or imagine a show that's staged as a carnival circus, like the one the wild Leatherette designers Richie Rich and Traver Rains once

presented. Some shows, like the recent one by French genius Jean Paul Gaultier, feature live animals. Another time, this innovative designer staged a giant puppet show, complete with puppeteer and "live" puppets! Pop-star-turned-designer Gwen Stefani presented a show in which the models emerged from old vintage cars. The great John Galliano of Dior fame once masterminded a spectacular catwalk filled with Chinese acrobats and a mammoth dancing dragon. One of his more recent runways featured a horse and vintage carriage. The brilliant hat designer Philip Treacy once hosted a show at a nightclub theater in which the models rose out of the stage floor. I've attended fashion shows staged on beaches, in train stations, on rooftops, in underground garages, in abandoned churches, parks, penthouses, old prisons, and even a former mental hospital! In fashion, there's never an end to imaginative ideas. And it's those amazing fashion show producers who make them all happen.

The Dressers

In fashion, there's a famous saying: "God is in the details." Nowhere is that more evident than in the realm of the dressers — those patient and organized men and women who have the crazy, often stressful, but satisfying job of ensuring that the models get their outfits on properly, with each and every accessory intact.

New York's Audrey Smaltz, a former model who's worked in every facet of the industry — from retail to styling to journalism to fashion show production — operates The Ground Crew, a company that supplies and organizes dressers for some of New York's top designer shows. She says that before she started her company, family and friends were dressing models because designers and producers felt there was no need for professionals in the backstage dressing rooms, other than designers and their assistants. But as the spectacle of the fashion show grew, with the increasing media focus, designers began to realize that they couldn't depend on "amateurs" for that all-important job of preparing the models. The Ground Crew dressers all have some fashion background and are trained in seminars before they work their first show. The clothes and accessories are laid out for them, usually with Polaroid pictures of the girls in the outfits from preshow fittings, so that each dresser knows exactly how his or her girl is going to look. Every detail is important — from shoelaces to belts to the designer's preference of which hand the bag goes in.

"Attention to detail is key," says Audrey. "You also have to work well with people and be able to roll with the punches. And you have to know how to mind your own business!" Crazy things can go down in those frantic backstage moments where everybody's often rushed and nerves are on end. Dressers have to be cool and refrain from gossiping – the rule of thumb in most jobs in fashion, especially when dealing with so many famous people who are under so much pressure.

Fashion Show Producer
KEVIN KRIER

Born in Red Wing, Minnesota, Kevin Krier was a theater arts major at Macalester College in St. Paul. He started a summer theater group, Songbird, in the Park, in his hometown. His first fashion job was as an assistant fashion editor at *Twin* magazine, and he went on to become the fashion director of the Men's Fashion Association. In 1985, he launched Kevin Krier and Associates, a public relations firm specializing in fashion show production.

Krier's client roster includes Gucci, Yves St. Laurent, Dolce & Gabbana, Stella McCartney, Tommy Hilfiger, Hugo Boss, and Diesel. He also has produced many legendary events, including awards for the AIDS Project Los Angeles (APLA), honoring *In Vogue* director Tom Ford in 1993. Created the Fashion for Relief star-studded runway spectacle as benefit for victims of Hurricane Katrina.

WORKING THE LOOK

The inspired mastery of stylists, hairstylists, and makeup artists

There are many people who perform magic in the wondrous world of fashion, but the stylists, makeup artists, and hairstylists are the real "Merlins" – masters of illusion who, through years of studying techniques and experimenting with different looks, manage to transform models into those captivating creatures that play starring roles in a designer's fantasies.

The Stylist

Like many of the players in the fashion world today, stylists – long considered to be the unsung heroes of the scene for helping a designer refine his or her vision – have become celebrities in their own rite. Many famous stylists, like Hollywood's Phillip Bloch, have made names for themselves by dressing celebrities for photo shoots, the red carpet, and other high-profile events. Phillip, who worked as a model for years before becoming a stylist, studied fashion at New York's FIT (Fashion Institute of Technology), but claims the best "training" is in the field. "Your connections are everything in this business," he notes. But besides having the connections that will win you the coveted assignments and the trust of top designers, editors, photographers, and perhaps even celebrities, you must have a broad knowledge of the fashion business, a deep understanding of the way clothes work, and great taste. "Besides modeling, I worked in fashion PR and retail," explains Phillip. "You have to know about people's body types, and you have to know about psychology – how to handle people – and how to even take measurements! I even worked as a designer for a period, so I learned how to cut patterns and what fabric can do. Styling isn't a beginning job. Some people think, 'Well, I have good taste, I like to shop, and I've got a credit card, so I'm going to be a stylist!' Well, that's the worst . . . I think you should work at a design house, you should work at a magazine, you should do PR – you should do all these other jobs and *then* go be a stylist. That's how you can be the best."

Of course, no two paths in the fashion business are ever the same. Everybody has their own experiences and there are no "set" ways to achieve success. The most important factor, though, especially when it comes to styling, is to have a passion for the clothes themselves and a strong viewpoint of how they should be worn. That being said, if you're working closely with a celebrity, you'll have to take his or her own comfort level into consideration. While many stylists have certainly helped transform celebrities and given them a strong sense of style, you don't want to impose your own style sense on someone who doesn't feel right about it. It's a tough challenge: If you dress an actress for the red carpet, and everybody loves what she's wearing, you're a hero! But if her outfit gets bad reviews by the critics, the stylist is often to blame.

Stylist
Todd Lynn

*B*orn in Smiths Falls, Ontario, Todd Lynn studied drama at the School of Performing Arts in Ottawa from 1983 to 1987. He then enrolled in the fashion program at Ryerson in Toronto, where he graduated in 1991. Lynn has worked with various Toronto designers as a pattern-cutter and a technical advisor. He has designed wardrobes for rock stars, such as Marilyn Manson; Bono; PJ Harvey; and Mick Jagger, Keith Richards, and Ronnie Wood of the Rolling Stones.

In 1998, Lynn enrolled in the fashion M.A. program at Central Saint Martins College in London. After completing his degree in 2000, he worked for London-based designer Roland Mouret as his technical designer and right-hand man. Lynn launched his own menswear label in 2006.

Being a stylist requires a lot of running around – and "schlepping." You're constantly borrowing clothes and accessories, so you – and your assistant, if you're lucky enough to have one – need to visit countless showrooms and stores, lugging stuff around. It's also important to attend as many fashion shows as possible, to see what's new. If you're working for a magazine shoot, you're working far in advance of when the photos will appear. You've got to know your trends inside out and creatively try to take what you're doing to some higher level – put your own "stamp" on it – or your looks will be just a carbon copy of someone else's. At magazines, you'll have to work closely with the publication's fashion director or editor and take the story they want to tell, and

their input, into account. Then you'll go on a mission to borrow all the clothes and accessories you'll need.

If you're just working closely with a photographer, you'll want him or her to approve the clothes you've chosen as well as your ideas for dressing the model. The collaboration between stylist and photographer usually happens in the studio before the shoot starts, when the model's having hair and makeup done. It's your responsibility to have all the clothes pressed, or steamed, and ready to go. If a photographer doesn't like the look of what he or she is shooting, it's unlikely anyone will get a good picture. Options are the name of the game when it comes to styling! A good stylist makes sure there is lots to choose from and knows how to "mix it up" in exciting ways.

The Hairstylist

Hairstylists are often saviors in fashion — a hairdo can make or break a look. They have to be well trained and understand the techniques, equipment, and products necessary when working with hair. There are many good hairstyling schools that will teach you the basics, but experience, once again, is key. Of course, jobs at hair salons are abundant — everybody always seems to be looking for a great hairdresser. And some hairdressers with their own salons have made very big names for themselves. Think of the famous Vidal Sassoon: In London, in the "Swingin' '60s," he revolutionized the fashion direction of hair with a single geometric haircut. Some hairdressers gain celebrity status by working with stars and giving them hairdos that become megatrendy. Hairstylists must be up on all things fashionable and be working on creative solutions to make people more beautiful *and* noticeable.

Hairstylists in the high-fashion world are especially innovative. And they work under tremendous pressure sometimes, especially backstage at fashion shows, where large numbers of girls are being sent to them in a short time frame. Usually, a whole team of hairdressers work together at the shows, under the direction of one head hairstylist. He or she works closely with the designer and the makeup artist, coming up with the signature hair "look" that will be right for each show. Often, these stylists use wigs or hair extensions to make the girls' hairdos consistent with one another's. Technique is key in knowing how to create these sometimes complicated looks.

Hairstylists should be mild mannered, patient, and consoling to their clients or the models they're working on, as stress levels can run high at fashion shows or shoots. It's important for a hairstylist to gain the trust of the person he or she is working on.

When it comes to photography jobs, a hairstylist could be asked to do many things. If the assignment is for a magazine, it's called an "editorial" and usually features a strong viewpoint. The hairstylist is expected to come up with creative concepts. Of course, he or she would consult closely with the magazine's fashion or beauty editor and perhaps even with the stylist on the shoot, ensuring the hairstyle goes with the clothes and jibes with the fashion story.

For work that's more "commercial," – doing hair for catalogs, or perhaps TV commercials – the hairstylist usually works more independently, collaborating with the makeup artist, but not going "over the top" – after all, nobody wants to be upstaged by their own hairdo, especially when the clothes are more "realistic" than what might be offered on a fantasy runway, or in a highly artistic editorial spread.

The Makeup Artist

Makeup artists are also key players in the fashion world, responsible for producing a very special magic. Technique is ultraimportant in makeup, and there are countless reputable makeup schools. But experimentation is also mandatory, and, again, experience counts big time. Makeup artists are in constant demand – at beauty salons, in film and television studios, for photographic shoots, and at fashion shows. Most makeup artists enjoy a multitude of work situations, where they can practice their creative and technical skills in a variety of ways. Some even train as hairdressers, so that productions with a lower budget can get away with hiring only one person to do the job of two. This hair/makeup duality is becoming increasingly popular on photo shoots, where producers often attempt to keep costs down.

Most makeup artists that I know have had a lifelong love of their art, and have been applying makeup on their friends and family as long as they can remember. But some start out as fine artists, like the brilliant British makeup artist Pat McGrath, who collaborates with

> "When you touch someone's face, it's like instant intimacy. And you really have to trust somebody to let them get that close to your face. It really does lend itself to a very cozy, intimate setting. Or it can be just the opposite. It can be a terrifying situation when you're having to work with someone that you feel is just not into it at all, and you're having to touch them. . . . You just have to detach yourself from the situation, and be a professional, and do what you have to do."
> — KEVYN AUCOIN, MAKEUP ARTIST

some of the world's most famous designers – Giorgio Armani, Valentino, and John Galliano – creating unique looks for their runways and, in the process, starting new makeup trends. "It's a wonderful feeling seeing a look I created for a show being featured as the next trend in makeup, and realizing what an influence my ideas have on the fashion industry and how women wear makeup," she says. Pat admits she always loved makeup growing up, and enjoyed shopping for cosmetics with her stylish mom. She even made her own face creams! But she didn't realize she could really turn that passion into a proper "job" until she started going to art school and hanging around at nightclubs. At the clubs, she met people from the industry and eventually fell into the fashion scene. Oddly enough, she never studied makeup formally, even though she's considered one of the best makeup artists in the world today. "I think having passion and determination for creating and exploring every aspect of makeup design is crucial to being a great makeup artist," she says.

Makeup Artist
PAT McGRATH

*B*orn in Northampton, England, Pat McGrath studied at art school. While out clubbing in London, she met stylist Kim Bowen, who helped guide her career. Self-taught, McGrath began doing makeup for London's *I.D.* magazine's fashion shoots. Since then, she has developed cosmetics for Aveda, Shisheido, and Armani, and catwalk makeup for such houses as Gucci, Yohji Yamamoto, Christian Dior, Dolce & Gabbana, Versace, John Galliano, and Viktor & Rolf. She also collaborated on ad campaigns for Versace, Valentino, Prada, and Calvin Klein. McGrath has worked with top photographers, including Steven Meisel, for Italian and American *Vogue* and *W Magazine*, and she has been sought out by celebrities such as Madonna, Jennifer Lopez, Christina Aguilera, Oprah Winfrey, Cameron Diaz, Sarah Jessica Parker, Gwyneth Paltrow, and Nicole Kidman. McGrath dispenses expert advice in *Allure* magazine, and she is the beauty director for *I.D.* magazine as well as the creative director for Procter & Gamble Beauty.

"The skill and technique can be learned and improved upon with experience, but you really have to love playing and having fun with makeup. . . . It's also very important to have extensive knowledge of history, art, literature, and current events – they will be constant sources of inspiration and reference to you." Pat also has these sage words of advice: "Don't be afraid to try new things and make mistakes; it comes with the territory and only makes your skills stronger and more inventive."

The late great makeup artist Kevyn Aucoin, for example, discovered a unique technique when he applied makeup to models and celebrities as they were lying down on the floor! He treated each face as a canvas, and he'd get down on the floor himself, studying each face and turning it into a living work of art. He did my makeup in this unconventional manner once, and it was one of the most memorable experiences I've ever had. He truly made me look and feel more beautiful than ever before. But Kevyn's work always went beyond the mere makeup. He had an uncanny way of connecting with all the people he worked on and making them feel special. And that, I know, was his biggest reward: profoundly touching his subjects and having an intimate and soulful connection with each and every woman that he transformed so magically.

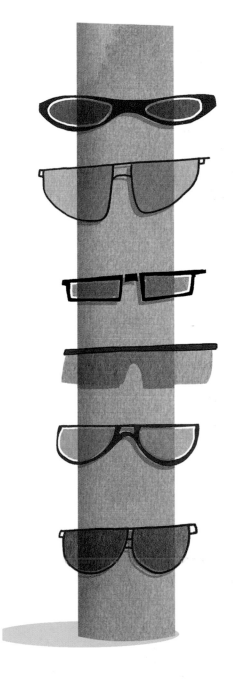

9 STYLE SPECULATION

Trend forecasters, color specialists, and personal shoppers:
Deciphering what's hot

The Trend Forecaster

It's often been said that great minds think alike. Maybe that explains why so many of fashion's great innovators seem to come out with the some of the same ideas around the same time. I'm always amazed at this "collective consciousness" in fashion, when similar trends crop up on a variety of international runways simultaneously. But who dictates these trends or approaches? Or are they simply reflections of attitudes in society? Consulting with fashion design and marketing companies, the business of analyzing trends and projecting which ones may be looming in our future is the domain of the trend forecaster. He or she is a kind of cultural anthropologist, and a multitude of fashion enterprises, including retailers and advertisers as well as textile designers and cosmetic companies, rely on these forecasters to help them dream up "the next big thing."

To be a trend forecaster, you have to have an intellectual understanding of fashion and its role in society. You have to be extremely aware of the world around you and have a natural curiosity about why people want to wear what they wear. David Wolfe of The Doneger Group, a New York based consulting company, is one of America's most respected forecasters. He began his specialized job in the early '70s. Before that, there wasn't a need for such a service because the Paris couture designers dictated the fashion direction. David, who began his career as a fashion illustrator, now travels a great deal, observing what people buy and wear, and he attends countless fashion shows. Most of his time is spent meeting with people in the industry: designers, buyers, and retailers. "I then assimilate and analyze all the information I've gathered and try to see the future. I work about eighteen to twenty-four months ahead of the current season," explains David.

As with most jobs in the industry, there's no one path to realizing your dream. David, for example, learned "on the job" – and he had a great many jobs in the industry: from artist to buyer to fashion show producer to makeup artist to photographer to journalist. That well-rounded background helped him develop into the great communicator that he is, running around the globe giving speeches and communicating his insightful ideas about where fashion is going.

The Color Specialist

Another consulting job (like that of the trend forecaster) is the job of color specialist. This unusual career depends on an individual's true passion for color and fascination with the psychology of color – discovering what colors mean to us and how they affect our moods and psyche. While designers, for the most part, choose their own colors, the analysis of why certain colors crop up in fashion is what

Color Specialist
LEATRICE EISEMAN

Born in Baltimore, Maryland, Leatrice Eiseman studied psychology at Antioch University. She received her counseling specialist certificate from UCLA. Eiseman has studied and taught fashion and interior design. She is the executive director of The Pantone Color Institute and the founder of The Eiseman Center for Color Information and Training. She has authored six books on color, including *The Color Answer Book, Colors For Your Every Mood*, and *More Alive with Color*.

Eiseman appears frequently as a guest on various TV shows, and she has been interviewed extensively in the written media as a color expert. She conducts seminars at trade shows, schools, design centers, and individual companies on the emotional impact of color, consumer response research, and color trends.

many books on the subject of color and consults for a variety of companies, helping them choose colors for products, packaging, and interiors. Leatrice says you obviously have to have an eye for color – and those that have it know it, even when they're children. "They're the kind of kids who love to play with crayons, and do creative things, and put colors together. I can remember my mother saying that when I was a little girl, I wouldn't go outside the house unless my socks, my hair ornaments, and everything else I was wearing went together. I was just so sensitive to color, like an artist," Leatrice reveals. While there's no formal training to be a color specialist, Leatrice suggests taking as many classes in color as possible and read everything you can about it.

many companies are interested in when it comes to creating their own trendy products. Leatrice Eiseman is a famous color specialist and the director of The Pantone Color Institute. She's written

> "The key to being a good personal shopper is to understand the client's needs and desires. I spend a lot of time discussing my client's lifestyle. . . . Each client is different and I customize each shopping trip. Sometimes my clients don't know what they are looking for. They want to change their look and I can help them do that . . . everyone has their own personal style and shouldn't try to be a fashion victim.
>
> — SUSAN TABAK, PERSONAL SHOPPER

politicians subscribe to the services of a style or image consultant to help them project a little more forcefully and memorably.

While a formal education may not be necessary to excel at image consulting, a solid background in different areas of fashion and a good understanding of psychology and business certainly help.

The Image Consultant

Some things in fashion just come naturally to some people. Take good taste — and a flare for style. They're very hard to cultivate if you don't have a natural feel for fashion. That's why more and more professional women and men — and even entire companies — are seeking the services of style or image consultants. These experts try to impart to their clients a keen sense of awareness and sensitivity toward sartorial esthetics. Personal image is extremely important in show business, big business, and politics, and many movie and music stars, high-powered businessmen, and

The Personal Shopper

Many people who don't have time to shop, an adequate sense of what looks good on them, or what they even like, employ the services of a personal shopper. These shoppers tirelessly scour stores and showrooms on a professional mission to dress a certain individual. Personal shoppers have a solid understanding of their client's tastes and body type, and bring that client all kinds of options to choose from, whether it's a wardrobe for work or a fabulous creation for a special event.

New York's Susan Tabak, a one-time assistant buyer at a big department store, is a personal shopper who specializes in Paris shopping. She claims she knows the city "inside out," and she speaks French. Susan goes to Paris several times a year, attends fashion shows, and visits a variety of chic shops, looking for "just the right thing" for her clients. "I think to be a great personal shopper," says Susan, "you need to be clever in helping your clients try new ideas — not necessarily change their look, but enhance it." Once again, there may not be any formal training or particular educational background necessary to be a personal shopper, but you can probably see in your own life that some people are just better at shopping than others. Some certainly love it more than others. It's that passion that's necessary to excel at anything you do in fashion. And it's that's passion, coupled with hard work, that will ultimately make you a success.

10 WHAT'S IN STORE

The creative and challenging business of retail

The Retailer

It's all very well for fashion's creative set to be dreaming fantastic dreams. And while some of those dreams are ultimately meant to inspire us, unless they can be translated into some form of reality, the "dreaming" can get very expensive and can't continue. Enter the retailers – those men and women who merchandise designer dreams. They try to ensure that the masses – or, at least a healthy number of people – buy into those dreams. Fashion retail environments – from big glitzy department stores to tiny, charming boutiques; from funky markets or bazaars to hip Internet sites that sell clothing, accessories, and cosmetics – are becoming increasingly exciting, eclectic, and stimulating settings for consumers, designers, and marketers. Ideally, these retail enterprises are the true acid test in the fashion business. They dictate a designer's success: If an idea doesn't sell, it's back to the drawing board – or sketch pad! Unless you have unlimited funds, no one in the fashion industry can survive if they can't sell their products to the public.

The Special Events Coordinator and The Marketing Director

Over the past twenty years, department stores that specialize in fashion have changed dramatically. No longer mere purveyors of merchandise, department stores around the world now desperately try to sell us style attitudes, sensibilities, and excitement. More and more, they're becoming entertainment emporiums, complete with a schedule of special events, such as fashion shows, seminars, demonstrations, cocktail parties, and "trunk shows" – those "meet the designer" presentations where customers can check out, try on, and order pieces from a collection. They often get acquainted with the actual designer responsible, or one of the design label's representatives. These in-store trunk shows are invaluable for designers, who crave direct feedback from those who wear their clothing. All these special events hosted by department stores require much organization and planning, so the big fashion department stores employ special events coordinators. They work alongside the stores' marketing directors to come up with original and creative ways to appeal to the public and get them into the stores in the first place.

Most retailers feel a deep responsibility to their customers: They want to educate them and make them feel that they care about them beyond just doing business. Today's retail environment is incredibly competitive – everybody's vying for your business, and retailers are intent on cultivating a certain loyalty from their customers. That's why, beyond the old-fashioned catalog, many high-end fashion retailers are publishing exclusive glossy magazines that are sent out to their customers, with beautiful editorial spreads featuring the store's merchandise, as well as engaging articles on style and

interviews with the designers behind the labels. Some stores employ full-time staff to work on these magazines. Usually, it's the store's creative director at the helm of these informative publications.

The Fashion Director

Some of the larger stores also have fashion directors. They are responsible for getting a global perspective on exactly what is happening in the world of fashion and bringing that information back to the store. Toronto's Barbara Atkin, the fashion director of Canada's prestigious Holt Renfrew chain, acts as a consultant who partners with the stores' buyers. These buyers travel the world, bringing back

> "It takes a lot of conviction in your beliefs to be a great fashion director and an ability to analyze long-term sociological trends, with an understanding of how social change will impact your business and lifestyle needs. You must be passionate, a great seller of ideas . . . able to think quickly . . . a great editor, a motivator, a great public speaker, and a fast decision maker."
> – BARBARA ATKIN, fashion director, Holt Renfrew

the name of Wayne Clark. They ended up in business together and began selling Wayne's stunning creations to Holt's. Barbara's relationship with Holt's eventually lured her to become their fashion director.

The late much-beloved Kal Ruttenstein, the former fashion director for the famous American chain Bloomingdale's, demonstrated how powerful a fashion director can be. He launched the careers of some of today's most successful designers, including Donna Karan and Marc Jacobs. The deep passion that Kal had for fashion was legendary: For years after he'd had a debilitating stroke and could not walk unassisted, he continued to travel the world and attend countless fashion shows. He may have slowed down tremendously on a physical level, but his personal drive and extraordinary love for fashion, and the designers who create it, kept him going.

those items they think their customers will want. They have to attend a variety of fashion shows and constantly visit designer showrooms to see the collections up close and to place their orders. "Buyers are responsible for their business in the present and are always looking at what's selling at the moment," explains Barbara. "The fashion director forecasts the 'newness' and opens the buyers' eyes as to where the new fashion direction will be, before the buyer gets to market to actually 'do the buy.' The fashion director is much like a teacher, and the buyer is her student." In fact, Barbara started out as a schoolteacher, until she met an exciting Canadian designer by

The Display Manager

At their best, large fashion department stores are theatrical environments where we go not only to shop, but to be entertained. That's why the role of display manager is so important. These people have a multitude of talents and work with imaginative teams of people to dress the store's windows and mannequins and fabricate arresting displays within the store to inspire people. Many store display managers have strong design and graphic art backgrounds, and many have been set designers. Obviously, an art school background, coupled with a deep love and understanding of fashion, is key to a display manager's success.

The Sales Staff

But the real champions in the world of fashion are the salespeople – those men and women who literally "get the product out there" by putting the designer dreams into the hands of the public. Inevitably, they make a lot of people happy, from the person purchasing the item to the store that's selling it to the designer who's created it. Without good sales staff, the fashion business couldn't survive. Interestingly, even though great, experienced salespeople are the mainstay of the business, the job of a salesperson on the floor can be a great entry-level position into the fashion world because it offers the perfect initial education about the realities of the business. By learning what customers want and need, by becoming familiar with various labels and products, and by discovering how important a role fashion can play in a person's life – either by elevating their mood, making them feel better about themselves, or helping them achieve a successful image – you'll have helped yourself lay the groundwork for a multitude of jobs within the industry.

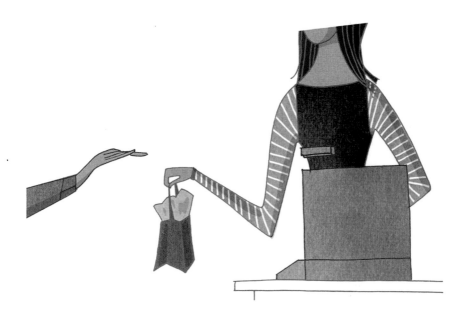

*B*orn in Toronto, Ontario, Barbara Atkin has a B.A. in social sciences from York University. She completed the marketing/advertising course at Ryerson University, and she received an Ontario Teachers Certificate from Toronto Teachers College. From 1971 to 1978, she worked as a teacher, devising a curriculum for new Canadians entering the Toronto school system. From 1978 to 1984, she was a partner at Aline Marelle Ltd., a fashion manufacturing company. Her responsibilities included assisting eveningwear designer Wayne Clark as a creative consultant, merchandising the line, running the showroom, developing the international ad campaigns, and doing all the marketing, PR, and special events. She was then a partner of Model Corp., where her duties included manufacturing, marketing, and wholesaling a variety of lines to Canadian retailers. From 1984 to 1987, she was a partner with Vizibility, where she handled PR, marketing, and special events for Canadian designers. Atkin has been the fashion director of Canada's upscale fashion chain, Holt Renfrew, for over twenty years.

And while sticking with the job of a salesperson might be satisfying enough, it's also bound to open many doors.

My very first job in fashion was as a salesperson at a Toronto women's clothing store, when I was sixteen years old! I learned firsthand that good salespeople have to be motivated, on their toes, and sensitive to the needs — and moods — of their customers. They have to have good taste and be as honest as possible: Nobody wants to be "talked into" something just because somebody wants to make a sale. Sales staff must know their product, have a lot of patience, delight in being helpful, be good communicators, and, most importantly, have a real love of people. After all, isn't that what fashion's ultimately about?

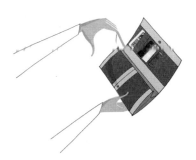

FASHION SCHOOLS

United States

Academy of Art University
www.academyart.edu
info@academyart.edu

79 New Montgomery Street
4th Floor
San Francisco, CA 94105-3410
USA
(800) 544-2787 (within US only)
or (415) 274-2200

Otis College of Art and Design
www.otis.edu
admissions@otis.edu

9045 Lincoln Boulevard
Los Angeles, CA 90045
USA

(800) 527-6847 or
(310) 665-6800

*Fashion Institute of Design and
Merchandising (FIDM)*
www.fidm.com

FIDM − Los Angeles Campus
919 South Grand Avenue
Los Angeles, CA 90015-1421
USA

(800) 624-1200 or
(213) 624-1201

*Also has campuses in Orange County, ·
San Francisco, and San Diego

Fashion Institute of Technology (FIT)
www.fitnyc.edu

Seventh Avenue at 27 Street
New York, NY 10001-5992
USA

(212) 217-7999

Parsons the New School for Design
www.parsons.edu
studentinfo@newschool.edu

65 Fifth Ave.
New York, NY 10003-3003

(212) 229-8933

Canada

Ryerson School of Fashion
www.ryerson.ca/fashion
fshninfo@ryerson.ca

40 Gould Street
Toronto, ON
M5B 2K3
Canada

(416) 979-5333

*International Academy
of Design & Technology*
www.iadt.ca

*International Academy of Design &
Technology − Toronto*
39 John Street
Toronto, ON
M5V 3G6
Canada

(416) 922-3666

United Kingdom

*Central Saint Martins College
of Art and Design*
www.csm.arts.ac.uk
info@csm.arts.ac.uk

Southampton Row
London WC1B 4AP
UK

+44 (0) 20 7514 7023

London College of Fashion
www.fashion.arts.ac.uk
enquiries@fashion.arts.ac.uk

20 John Princes Street
London W1G 0BJ
UK

+44 (0) 20 7514 7407

Belgium

*Antwerp Royal Academy of Fine
Arts − Hogeschool Antwerp*
www.antwerp-fashion.be
mode@ha.be

Hogeschool Antwerp, Fashion
Department
Nationalestraat 28/3
2000 Antwerp
Belgium

+32 3 206 08 80

Italy

Istituto Marangoni
www.istitutomarangoni.com
t.lancellotti@istitutomarangoni.com

Via Verri, 4
20121 Milan
Italy

+39 02 7631 6680

*This is where Domenico Dolce studied
*Also has campuses in London and Paris

*Polimoda International Institute of
Fashion Design and Marketing*
www.polimoda.com
info@polimoda.com

Polimoda
Villa Strozzi
Via Pisana, 77
50143 Firenze
Italy

+39 055 7399628

Netherlands

*Hogeschool van Amsterdam −
Amsterdam Fashion Institute (AMFI)*
www.amfi.hva.nl
studievoorlichting@hva.nl

Binnengasthuisstraat 9
1012 ZA Amsterdam
Netherlands

+31 (0) 20 525 67 77

France

*ESMOD International Fashion
Design School*
www.esmod.com
paris@esmod.com

12, rue de la Rochefoucauld
75009 Paris
France

+33 (0) 1 44 83 81 50

Ecole Lesage (Atelier de Broderie)
www.lesage-paris.com
ecole-lesage@wanadoo.fr

13, rue de la Grange Batelière
75009 Paris
France

+33 (0) 1 44 79 00 88

Spain

Centro Superior Diseno de Moda
www.csdmm.upm.es
inform.csdmm@upm.es

Carretera de Valencia, km, 7
Campus Sur de la UPM
Bloque I, planta Baja
28031 Madrid
Spain

+91 331 01 26

Japan

Bunka Fashion College
www.bunka-fc.ac.jp

3-22-1, Yoyogi
Shibuya-ku, Tokyo
151-8522
Japan

+81-(0) 3-3299-2057

*Kenzo Takada and Yohji Yamamoto
studied here